Dr Jack

Third Illus

SOUTH AFRICAN BYRD BOOK

WOOLLY-NECKED STORK

Ciconia episcopus

CW00601237

FOREWORD

I am fascinated by the creative urge: that moment, perhaps first captured in the caves of Altamira, when one of our Palaeolithic ancestors spread his artistic palm against the wall and blew ochre dust over it, leaving a silhouette of his hand for eternity. Among the many beautiful pictures of animals, it is the hand print that stays with me; the stone-age equivalent of 'Kilroy was here'.

Artists are different. If you don't believe me, you should meet Dr Jack. If there is a gentler human being on the face of the planet I have yet to meet him. He is particularly fond of snakes and all manner of crawling things, seeing them as we never do, art in motion. But when he is staring out of his studio window, more often than not it is the sky that grabs his attention.

Within these pages you will discover why Dr Jack tends to look up instead of down. It is in the hope of spotting – and perhaps swapping ideas with – a greater painted snipe. It is a search for the inspiration of a pun on the run, or, in ornithological terms, a whim on the wing. For, unlike our Palaeolithic artist, with Dr Jack there is always a deadline to consider.

Charles M Schultz, the creator of 'Peanuts', used to work six weeks in advance. He figured that if he should be incapacitated, the strip could run in the papers while he was in hospital and no one would be any the wiser. But his family never understood his self-imposed deadline and would interrupt him, for no good reason, if they saw him standing around in his studio.

So he had an annex built on his house, where he would go to draw and think. The masterstroke was that he added a covered walkway from the house to the studio and whenever he heard someone coming down it he would immediately leap into his chair, grab his pencil and start drawing furiously. The interloper would see him through the window in the door (masterstroke number two) and turn back, rather than interrupt him.

He explained to his biographer, 'They don't understand that when I'm staring out of the window, that's as hard as I ever work'.

So if you haven't had the privilege of watching Dr Jack at work, think of Schultz and remember that art is 1% drawing and 99% daydreaming. South Africa's premier illustrator has been entertaining us for over a quarter century now, and for the majority of that time his many editors have held to the mantra, 'We don't want it good, we want it Tuesday'.

Some years ago we were introduced via the internet by a friend we had in common. I had scribbled a Christmas story that defied photographic illustration, and so our friend involved Dr Jack. Over the next two years we collaborated on a series of short stories set in the mythical dorp of Ystervarkrivier. There were times when inspiration was as far away from me as Peru, when it was purely the thought of Dr Jack's eventual picture that kept me going.

It was Douglas Adams who said, 'I love deadlines. I like the whooshing sound they make as they fly by'. He would never have made it in journalism. Adams' publisher once locked him in a hotel room and put a guard on the door to force him to write. Dr Jack goes into the room voluntarily and, almost every day, produces something worthwhile; in a word, art.

Where does it come from? Almost always from the last place you'd expect. Hollywood churns out sequels and prequels on the basis that, 'It worked last time'. There is a horror of the new, a fear that the public won't like it. But the artist has to live on the edge between courting public acceptance and avoiding it like the plague. After all, in the wise words of ee cummings, 'Popularity is the hallmark of mediocrity'.

So every day Dr Jack goes to the well in the hope that there will be inspiration within. He has made a rod for his own back and his audience expects wit, wisdom and that indefinable extra something. And they expect it today, which might explain why it is that Dr Jack has waited 25 years to come up with the sequel to his two seminal 'byrd books'. He doesn't have enough space in his day.

It is not as though time has stood still, however. In the years dividing book two from book three, Dr Jack has chronicled South Africa's move from an apartheid state to a democracy, from FW de Klerk and PW Botha to Nelson Mandela and Jacob Zuma. His style has evolved and his eye has been honed. He has passed through the space reserved for crude pictures with speech bubbles and pushed through into the realm of fine art. To call Dr Jack a cartoonist is laughable, and much as we all enjoy a good laugh, he should be regarded in the same noble line as that of Cruickshank and Daumier, not Scott Adams and Jim Davis.

This book is what John James Audubon might have produced had he had a sense of humour and lived in Mpumalanga instead of Philadelphia. Long after you have finished smiling at the jokes, you will remember the pictures. I recommend it to you unreservedly.

ANDY CAPOSTAGNO
Lidgetton, KwaZulu-Natal

GARDEN WARBLER

Sylvia borin

ROSY-FACED LOVEBIRD
Agapornis roseicollis

KINGFISHER
Megaceryle maxima

AFRICAN SACRED IBIS
Threskiornis aethiopicus

EUROPEAN BEE-EATER

Merops apiaster

MARTIAL EAGLE
Polemaetus bellicosus

WESTERN CATTLE EGRET
Bubulcus ibis

BLACKSMITH LAPWING
Vanellus armatus

ALPINE SWIFT
Tachmarptis melba

RED KNOT
Calidris canutus
(subsp: *doublesheetbedicus*)

INDIAN YELLOW-NOSED ALBATROSS
Thalassarche carteri

SCARCE SWIFT
Schoutedenapus myoptilus

SOUTHERN MASKED WEAVER
Ploceus velatus #1

SOUTHERN MASKED WEAVER
Ploceus velatus #2

SPOTTED FLYCATCHER
Muscicapa striata

AFRICAN EMERALD CUCKOO
Chrysococcyx cupreus

PURPLE ROLLER
Coracias naevius

CLOUD CISTICOLA
Cisticola textrix

SOUTH AFRICAN SHEL(L)DUCK
Tadorna cana

BEARDED SCRUB ROBIN

Cercotrichas quadrivirgata

CROWNED LAPWING

Vanellus coronatus

CAPPED WHEATEAR
Oenanthe pileata

YELLOW-BELLIED EREMOMELA

Eremomela icteropygialis

CURLEW SANDPIPER
Calidris ferruginea

BLACK SAW-WING
Psalidoprocne holomelas

EASTERN LONG-BILLED LARK

Certhilauda semitorquata

STREAKY-HEADED SEEDEATER

Crithagra gularis

COMMON RINGED PLOVER
Charadrius hiaticula

TINY GREENBUL
Phyllastrephus debilis

COPPERY-TAILED COUCAL

Centropus cupreicaudus

GREEN MALKOHA

Ceuthmochares aereus

CAPE ROCKJUMPER
Chaetops frenatus

HOUSE CROW

Corvus splendens

BLACK-FACED WAXBILL
Estrilda erythronotos

TINKLING CISTICOLA
Cisticola rufilatus

COLLARED SUNBIRD
Hedydipna collaris
and
COPPER SUNBIRD
Cinnyris cupreus

CAPE SHOVELER

Anas smithii (semase)

RED-NECKED SPURFOWL

Pternistis afer

SPOTTED THICK-KNEE
Burhinus capensis

WATER THICK-KNEE
Burhinus vermiculatus

HARLEQUIN QUAIL
Coturnix delegorguei

CARDINAL WOODPECKER
Dendropicos fuscescens

GREATER PAINTED-SNIPE

Rostratula benghalensis

BANK CORMORANT
Phalacrocorax neglectus

LONG- ~~TAILED~~ TALED WIDOWBIRD

Euplectes progne

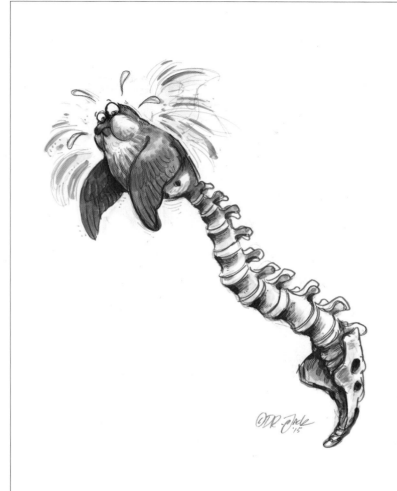

MOTTLED SPINETAIL
Telacanthura ussheri

AFRICAN CROWNED EAGLE

Stephanoaetus coronatus

AFRICAN SPOONBILL
Platalea alba

BAT HAWK
Macheiramphus alcinus

WHITE-STARRED ROBIN
Pogonocichla stellata

AFRICAN WOOD OWL
Strix woodfordii
and
GOLDEN-TAILED WOODPECKER
Campethera abingoni

WING-SNAPPING CISTICOLA
Cisticola ayresii

PIED AVO (CADO) CET

Recurvirostra avosetta

SADDLE-BILLED STORK
Ephippiorhynchus senegalensis

ROCK DOVE
Columbia livia

TRUMPETER HORNBILL

Bycanistes bucinator

GREAT CRESTED GREBE
Podiceps cristatus

CHORISTER ROBIN-CHAT
Cossypha dichroa

GREEN TINKERBIRD

Pogoniulus simplex

JACKAL BUZZARD
Buteo rufofuscus

BARE-CHEEKED BABBLER
Turdoides gymnogenys

AFRICAN GRASS OWL
Tyto capensis

MARICO SUNBIRD

Cinnyris mariquensis

ZITTING CISTICOLA
Cisticola juncidis

RED-THROATED WRYNECK
Jynx ruficollis

COMMON SCIMITARBILL
Rhinopomastus cyanomelas

RED-BILLED BUFFALO WEAVER
Bubalornis niger

GREY GO-AWAY-BIRD
Corythaixoides concolor

Published by Struik Nature (an imprint of
Penguin Random House South Africa (Pty) Ltd)
Reg. No. 1953/000441/07
The Estuaries No. 4, Oxbow Crescent,
Century Avenue, Century City, 7441
PO Box 1144, Cape Town, 8000 South Africa

Visit **www.penguinrandomhouse.co.za**
and join the Struik Nature Club
for updates, news, events and special offers.

1 3 5 7 9 10 8 6 4 2

Copyright © in illustrations and text, 2016: Dr Jack
Copyright © in published edition, 2016:
Penguin Random House South Africa (Pty) Ltd

Publisher: Pippa Parker
Typesetter: Deirdré Geldenhuys

Reproduction by Hirt & Carter Cape (Pty) Ltd
Printed and bound by DJE Flexible Print Solutions

All rights reserved. No part of this publication may be reproduced,
stored in a retrieval system or transmitted in any form or by any means,
electronic, mechanical, photocopying, recording or otherwise, without
the prior written permission of the publishers and copyright holders.

Print: 978 1 77584 528 7
ePub: 978 1 77584 553 9
ePDF: 978 1 77584 554 6

BANK CORMORANT
Phalacrocorax neglectus